The Movie Critic's Notebook

TITLE:

YEAR:

GENRE:

WHERE WATCHED:

DATE SEEN:

WHO WITH:

OVERALL SCORE:

☆ ☆ ☆ ☆ ☆

DIRECTOR:

☆ ☆ ☆ ☆ ☆

CAST:

☆ ☆ ☆ ☆ ☆

SCREENPLAY:

☆ ☆ ☆ ☆ ☆

CINEMATOGRAPHY:

☆ ☆ ☆ ☆ ☆

SPECIAL EFFECTS/ANIMATION:

☆ ☆ ☆ ☆ ☆

PRODUCTION DESIGN:

☆ ☆ ☆ ☆ ☆

MUSICAL SCORE:

☆ ☆ ☆ ☆ ☆

COSTUMING AND PROPS:

☆ ☆ ☆ ☆ ☆

NOTES:

TITLE:

YEAR:

GENRE:

WHERE WATCHED:

DATE SEEN:

WHO WITH:

OVERALL SCORE:
☆☆☆☆☆

DIRECTOR:
☆☆☆☆☆

CAST:
☆☆☆☆☆

SCREENPLAY:
☆☆☆☆☆

CINEMATOGRAPHY:
☆☆☆☆☆

SPECIAL EFFECTS/ANIMATION:
☆☆☆☆☆

PRODUCTION DESIGN:
☆☆☆☆☆

MUSICAL SCORE:
☆☆☆☆☆

COSTUMING AND PROPS:
☆☆☆☆☆

NOTES:

TITLE:

YEAR:

GENRE:

WHERE WATCHED:

DATE SEEN:

WHO WITH:

OVERALL SCORE:
☆ ☆ ☆ ☆ ☆

DIRECTOR:
☆ ☆ ☆ ☆ ☆

CAST:
☆ ☆ ☆ ☆ ☆

SCREENPLAY:
☆ ☆ ☆ ☆ ☆

CINEMATOGRAPHY:
☆ ☆ ☆ ☆ ☆

SPECIAL EFFECTS/ANIMATION:
☆ ☆ ☆ ☆ ☆

PRODUCTION DESIGN:
☆ ☆ ☆ ☆ ☆

MUSICAL SCORE:
☆ ☆ ☆ ☆ ☆

COSTUMING AND PROPS:
☆ ☆ ☆ ☆ ☆

NOTES:

TITLE:

YEAR:

GENRE:

WHERE WATCHED:

DATE SEEN:

WHO WITH:

OVERALL SCORE:
☆☆☆☆☆

DIRECTOR:
☆☆☆☆☆

CAST:
☆☆☆☆☆

SCREENPLAY:
☆☆☆☆☆

CINEMATOGRAPHY:
☆☆☆☆☆

SPECIAL EFFECTS/ANIMATION:
☆☆☆☆☆

PRODUCTION DESIGN:
☆☆☆☆☆

MUSICAL SCORE:
☆☆☆☆☆

COSTUMING AND PROPS:
☆☆☆☆☆

NOTES:

TITLE:

YEAR:

GENRE:

WHERE WATCHED:

DATE SEEN:

WHO WITH:

OVERALL SCORE:
☆ ☆ ☆ ☆ ☆

DIRECTOR:
☆ ☆ ☆ ☆ ☆

CAST:
☆ ☆ ☆ ☆ ☆

SCREENPLAY:
☆ ☆ ☆ ☆ ☆

CINEMATOGRAPHY:
☆ ☆ ☆ ☆ ☆

SPECIAL EFFECTS/ANIMATION:
☆ ☆ ☆ ☆ ☆

PRODUCTION DESIGN:
☆ ☆ ☆ ☆ ☆

MUSICAL SCORE:
☆ ☆ ☆ ☆ ☆

COSTUMING AND PROPS:
☆ ☆ ☆ ☆ ☆

NOTES:

TITLE:

YEAR:

GENRE:

WHERE WATCHED:

DATE SEEN:

WHO WITH:

OVERALL SCORE:
☆ ☆ ☆ ☆ ☆

DIRECTOR:
☆ ☆ ☆ ☆ ☆

CAST:
☆ ☆ ☆ ☆ ☆

SCREENPLAY:
☆ ☆ ☆ ☆ ☆

CINEMATOGRAPHY:
☆ ☆ ☆ ☆ ☆

SPECIAL EFFECTS/ANIMATION:
☆ ☆ ☆ ☆ ☆

PRODUCTION DESIGN:
☆ ☆ ☆ ☆ ☆

MUSICAL SCORE:
☆ ☆ ☆ ☆ ☆

COSTUMING AND PROPS:
☆ ☆ ☆ ☆ ☆

NOTES:

TITLE:

YEAR:

GENRE:

WHERE WATCHED:

DATE SEEN:

WHO WITH:

OVERALL SCORE:
☆ ☆ ☆ ☆ ☆

DIRECTOR:
☆ ☆ ☆ ☆ ☆

CAST:
☆ ☆ ☆ ☆ ☆

SCREENPLAY:
☆ ☆ ☆ ☆ ☆

CINEMATOGRAPHY:
☆ ☆ ☆ ☆ ☆

SPECIAL EFFECTS/ANIMATION:
☆ ☆ ☆ ☆ ☆

PRODUCTION DESIGN:
☆ ☆ ☆ ☆ ☆

MUSICAL SCORE:
☆ ☆ ☆ ☆ ☆

COSTUMING AND PROPS:
☆ ☆ ☆ ☆ ☆

NOTES:

TITLE:

YEAR:

GENRE:

WHERE WATCHED:

DATE SEEN:

WHO WITH:

OVERALL SCORE:
☆ ☆ ☆ ☆ ☆

DIRECTOR:
☆ ☆ ☆ ☆ ☆

CAST:
☆ ☆ ☆ ☆ ☆

SCREENPLAY:
☆ ☆ ☆ ☆ ☆

CINEMATOGRAPHY:
☆ ☆ ☆ ☆ ☆

SPECIAL EFFECTS/ANIMATION:
☆ ☆ ☆ ☆ ☆

PRODUCTION DESIGN:
☆ ☆ ☆ ☆ ☆

MUSICAL SCORE:
☆ ☆ ☆ ☆ ☆

COSTUMING AND PROPS:
☆ ☆ ☆ ☆ ☆

NOTES:

TITLE:

YEAR:

GENRE:

WHERE WATCHED:

DATE SEEN:

WHO WITH:

OVERALL SCORE:

☆ ☆ ☆ ☆ ☆

DIRECTOR:

☆ ☆ ☆ ☆ ☆

CAST:

☆ ☆ ☆ ☆ ☆

SCREENPLAY:

☆ ☆ ☆ ☆ ☆

CINEMATOGRAPHY:

☆ ☆ ☆ ☆ ☆

SPECIAL EFFECTS/ANIMATION:

☆ ☆ ☆ ☆ ☆

PRODUCTION DESIGN:

☆ ☆ ☆ ☆ ☆

MUSICAL SCORE:

☆ ☆ ☆ ☆ ☆

COSTUMING AND PROPS:

☆ ☆ ☆ ☆ ☆

NOTES:

TITLE:

YEAR:

GENRE:

WHERE WATCHED:

DATE SEEN:

WHO WITH:

OVERALL SCORE:
☆☆☆☆☆

DIRECTOR:
☆☆☆☆☆

CAST:
☆☆☆☆☆

SCREENPLAY:
☆☆☆☆☆

CINEMATOGRAPHY:
☆☆☆☆☆

SPECIAL EFFECTS/ANIMATION:
☆☆☆☆☆

PRODUCTION DESIGN:
☆☆☆☆☆

MUSICAL SCORE:
☆☆☆☆☆

COSTUMING AND PROPS:
☆☆☆☆☆

NOTES:

TITLE:

YEAR:

GENRE:

WHERE WATCHED:

DATE SEEN:

WHO WITH:

OVERALL SCORE:
☆ ☆ ☆ ☆ ☆

DIRECTOR:
☆ ☆ ☆ ☆ ☆

CAST:
☆ ☆ ☆ ☆ ☆

SCREENPLAY:
☆ ☆ ☆ ☆ ☆

CINEMATOGRAPHY:
☆ ☆ ☆ ☆ ☆

SPECIAL EFFECTS/ANIMATION:
☆ ☆ ☆ ☆ ☆

PRODUCTION DESIGN:
☆ ☆ ☆ ☆ ☆

MUSICAL SCORE:
☆ ☆ ☆ ☆ ☆

COSTUMING AND PROPS:
☆ ☆ ☆ ☆ ☆

NOTES:

TITLE:

YEAR:

GENRE:

WHERE WATCHED:

DATE SEEN:

WHO WITH:

OVERALL SCORE:
☆ ☆ ☆ ☆ ☆

DIRECTOR:
☆ ☆ ☆ ☆ ☆

CAST:
☆ ☆ ☆ ☆ ☆

SCREENPLAY:
☆ ☆ ☆ ☆ ☆

CINEMATOGRAPHY:
☆ ☆ ☆ ☆ ☆

SPECIAL EFFECTS/ANIMATION:
☆ ☆ ☆ ☆ ☆

PRODUCTION DESIGN:
☆ ☆ ☆ ☆ ☆

MUSICAL SCORE:
☆ ☆ ☆ ☆ ☆

COSTUMING AND PROPS:
☆ ☆ ☆ ☆ ☆

NOTES:

TITLE:

YEAR:

GENRE:

WHERE WATCHED:

DATE SEEN:

WHO WITH:

OVERALL SCORE:
☆ ☆ ☆ ☆ ☆

DIRECTOR:
☆ ☆ ☆ ☆ ☆

CAST:
☆ ☆ ☆ ☆ ☆

SCREENPLAY:
☆ ☆ ☆ ☆ ☆

CINEMATOGRAPHY:
☆ ☆ ☆ ☆ ☆

SPECIAL EFFECTS/ANIMATION:
☆ ☆ ☆ ☆ ☆

PRODUCTION DESIGN:
☆ ☆ ☆ ☆ ☆

MUSICAL SCORE:
☆ ☆ ☆ ☆ ☆

COSTUMING AND PROPS:
☆ ☆ ☆ ☆ ☆

NOTES:

TITLE:

YEAR:

GENRE:

WHERE WATCHED:

DATE SEEN:

WHO WITH:

OVERALL SCORE:
☆ ☆ ☆ ☆ ☆

DIRECTOR:
☆ ☆ ☆ ☆ ☆

CAST:
☆ ☆ ☆ ☆ ☆

SCREENPLAY:
☆ ☆ ☆ ☆ ☆

CINEMATOGRAPHY:
☆ ☆ ☆ ☆ ☆

SPECIAL EFFECTS/ANIMATION:
☆ ☆ ☆ ☆ ☆

PRODUCTION DESIGN:
☆ ☆ ☆ ☆ ☆

MUSICAL SCORE:
☆ ☆ ☆ ☆ ☆

COSTUMING AND PROPS:
☆ ☆ ☆ ☆ ☆

NOTES:

TITLE:

YEAR:

GENRE:

WHERE WATCHED:

DATE SEEN:

WHO WITH:

OVERALL SCORE:
☆ ☆ ☆ ☆ ☆

DIRECTOR:
☆ ☆ ☆ ☆ ☆

CAST:
☆ ☆ ☆ ☆ ☆

SCREENPLAY:
☆ ☆ ☆ ☆ ☆

CINEMATOGRAPHY:
☆ ☆ ☆ ☆ ☆

SPECIAL EFFECTS/ANIMATION:
☆ ☆ ☆ ☆ ☆

PRODUCTION DESIGN:
☆ ☆ ☆ ☆ ☆

MUSICAL SCORE:
☆ ☆ ☆ ☆ ☆

COSTUMING AND PROPS:
☆ ☆ ☆ ☆ ☆

NOTES:

TITLE:

YEAR:

GENRE:

WHERE WATCHED:

DATE SEEN:

WHO WITH:

OVERALL SCORE:
☆ ☆ ☆ ☆ ☆

DIRECTOR:
☆ ☆ ☆ ☆ ☆

CAST:
☆ ☆ ☆ ☆ ☆

SCREENPLAY:
☆ ☆ ☆ ☆ ☆

CINEMATOGRAPHY:
☆ ☆ ☆ ☆ ☆

SPECIAL EFFECTS/ANIMATION:
☆ ☆ ☆ ☆ ☆

PRODUCTION DESIGN:
☆ ☆ ☆ ☆ ☆

MUSICAL SCORE:
☆ ☆ ☆ ☆ ☆

COSTUMING AND PROPS:
☆ ☆ ☆ ☆ ☆

NOTES:

TITLE:

YEAR:

GENRE:

WHERE WATCHED:

DATE SEEN:

WHO WITH:

OVERALL SCORE:
☆ ☆ ☆ ☆ ☆

DIRECTOR:
☆ ☆ ☆ ☆ ☆

CAST:
☆ ☆ ☆ ☆ ☆

SCREENPLAY:
☆ ☆ ☆ ☆ ☆

CINEMATOGRAPHY:
☆ ☆ ☆ ☆ ☆

SPECIAL EFFECTS/ANIMATION:
☆ ☆ ☆ ☆ ☆

PRODUCTION DESIGN:
☆ ☆ ☆ ☆ ☆

MUSICAL SCORE:
☆ ☆ ☆ ☆ ☆

COSTUMING AND PROPS:
☆ ☆ ☆ ☆ ☆

NOTES:

TITLE:

YEAR:

GENRE:

WHERE WATCHED:

DATE SEEN:

WHO WITH:

OVERALL SCORE:
☆☆☆☆☆

DIRECTOR:
☆☆☆☆☆

CAST:
☆☆☆☆☆

SCREENPLAY:
☆☆☆☆☆

CINEMATOGRAPHY:
☆☆☆☆☆

SPECIAL EFFECTS/ANIMATION:
☆☆☆☆☆

PRODUCTION DESIGN:
☆☆☆☆☆

MUSICAL SCORE:
☆☆☆☆☆

COSTUMING AND PROPS:
☆☆☆☆☆

NOTES:

TITLE:

YEAR:

GENRE:

WHERE WATCHED:

DATE SEEN:

WHO WITH:

OVERALL SCORE:
☆ ☆ ☆ ☆ ☆

DIRECTOR:
☆ ☆ ☆ ☆ ☆

CAST:
☆ ☆ ☆ ☆ ☆

SCREENPLAY:
☆ ☆ ☆ ☆ ☆

CINEMATOGRAPHY:
☆ ☆ ☆ ☆ ☆

SPECIAL EFFECTS/ANIMATION:
☆ ☆ ☆ ☆ ☆

PRODUCTION DESIGN:
☆ ☆ ☆ ☆ ☆

MUSICAL SCORE:
☆ ☆ ☆ ☆ ☆

COSTUMING AND PROPS:
☆ ☆ ☆ ☆ ☆

NOTES:

TITLE:

YEAR:

GENRE:

WHERE WATCHED:

DATE SEEN:

WHO WITH:

OVERALL SCORE:
☆ ☆ ☆ ☆ ☆

DIRECTOR:
☆ ☆ ☆ ☆ ☆

CAST:
☆ ☆ ☆ ☆ ☆

SCREENPLAY:
☆ ☆ ☆ ☆ ☆

CINEMATOGRAPHY:
☆ ☆ ☆ ☆ ☆

SPECIAL EFFECTS/ANIMATION:
☆ ☆ ☆ ☆ ☆

PRODUCTION DESIGN:
☆ ☆ ☆ ☆ ☆

MUSICAL SCORE:
☆ ☆ ☆ ☆ ☆

COSTUMING AND PROPS:
☆ ☆ ☆ ☆ ☆

NOTES:

TITLE:

YEAR:

GENRE:

WHERE WATCHED:

DATE SEEN:

WHO WITH:

OVERALL SCORE:

☆ ☆ ☆ ☆ ☆

DIRECTOR:

☆ ☆ ☆ ☆ ☆

CAST:

☆ ☆ ☆ ☆ ☆

SCREENPLAY:

☆ ☆ ☆ ☆ ☆

CINEMATOGRAPHY:

☆ ☆ ☆ ☆ ☆

SPECIAL EFFECTS/ANIMATION:

☆ ☆ ☆ ☆ ☆

PRODUCTION DESIGN:

☆ ☆ ☆ ☆ ☆

MUSICAL SCORE:

☆ ☆ ☆ ☆ ☆

COSTUMING AND PROPS:

☆ ☆ ☆ ☆ ☆

NOTES:

TITLE:

YEAR:

GENRE:

WHERE WATCHED:

DATE SEEN:

WHO WITH:

OVERALL SCORE:
☆☆☆☆☆

DIRECTOR:
☆☆☆☆☆

CAST:
☆☆☆☆☆

SCREENPLAY:
☆☆☆☆☆

CINEMATOGRAPHY:
☆☆☆☆☆

SPECIAL EFFECTS/ANIMATION:
☆☆☆☆☆

PRODUCTION DESIGN:
☆☆☆☆☆

MUSICAL SCORE:
☆☆☆☆☆

COSTUMING AND PROPS:
☆☆☆☆☆

NOTES:

TITLE:

YEAR:

GENRE:

WHERE WATCHED:

DATE SEEN:

WHO WITH:

OVERALL SCORE:
☆ ☆ ☆ ☆ ☆

DIRECTOR:
☆ ☆ ☆ ☆ ☆

CAST:
☆ ☆ ☆ ☆ ☆

SCREENPLAY:
☆ ☆ ☆ ☆ ☆

CINEMATOGRAPHY:
☆ ☆ ☆ ☆ ☆

SPECIAL EFFECTS/ANIMATION:
☆ ☆ ☆ ☆ ☆

PRODUCTION DESIGN:
☆ ☆ ☆ ☆ ☆

MUSICAL SCORE:
☆ ☆ ☆ ☆ ☆

COSTUMING AND PROPS:
☆ ☆ ☆ ☆ ☆

NOTES:

TITLE:

YEAR:

GENRE:

WHERE WATCHED:

DATE SEEN:

WHO WITH:

OVERALL SCORE: ☆☆☆☆☆

DIRECTOR: ☆☆☆☆☆

CAST: ☆☆☆☆☆

SCREENPLAY: ☆☆☆☆☆

CINEMATOGRAPHY: ☆☆☆☆☆

SPECIAL EFFECTS/ANIMATION: ☆☆☆☆☆

PRODUCTION DESIGN: ☆☆☆☆☆

MUSICAL SCORE: ☆☆☆☆☆

COSTUMING AND PROPS: ☆☆☆☆☆

NOTES:

TITLE:

YEAR:

GENRE:

WHERE WATCHED:

DATE SEEN:

WHO WITH:

OVERALL SCORE:
☆ ☆ ☆ ☆ ☆

DIRECTOR:
☆ ☆ ☆ ☆ ☆

CAST:
☆ ☆ ☆ ☆ ☆

SCREENPLAY:
☆ ☆ ☆ ☆ ☆

CINEMATOGRAPHY:
☆ ☆ ☆ ☆ ☆

SPECIAL EFFECTS/ANIMATION:
☆ ☆ ☆ ☆ ☆

PRODUCTION DESIGN:
☆ ☆ ☆ ☆ ☆

MUSICAL SCORE:
☆ ☆ ☆ ☆ ☆

COSTUMING AND PROPS:
☆ ☆ ☆ ☆ ☆

NOTES:

TITLE:

YEAR:

GENRE:

WHERE WATCHED:

DATE SEEN:

WHO WITH:

OVERALL SCORE:
☆ ☆ ☆ ☆ ☆

DIRECTOR:
☆ ☆ ☆ ☆ ☆

CAST:
☆ ☆ ☆ ☆ ☆

SCREENPLAY:
☆ ☆ ☆ ☆ ☆

CINEMATOGRAPHY:
☆ ☆ ☆ ☆ ☆

SPECIAL EFFECTS/ANIMATION:
☆ ☆ ☆ ☆ ☆

PRODUCTION DESIGN:
☆ ☆ ☆ ☆ ☆

MUSICAL SCORE:
☆ ☆ ☆ ☆ ☆

COSTUMING AND PROPS:
☆ ☆ ☆ ☆ ☆

NOTES:

TITLE:

YEAR:

GENRE:

WHERE WATCHED:

DATE SEEN:

WHO WITH:

OVERALL SCORE:
☆ ☆ ☆ ☆ ☆

DIRECTOR:
☆ ☆ ☆ ☆ ☆

CAST:
☆ ☆ ☆ ☆ ☆

SCREENPLAY:
☆ ☆ ☆ ☆ ☆

CINEMATOGRAPHY:
☆ ☆ ☆ ☆ ☆

SPECIAL EFFECTS/ANIMATION:
☆ ☆ ☆ ☆ ☆

PRODUCTION DESIGN:
☆ ☆ ☆ ☆ ☆

MUSICAL SCORE:
☆ ☆ ☆ ☆ ☆

COSTUMING AND PROPS:
☆ ☆ ☆ ☆ ☆

NOTES:

TITLE:

YEAR:

GENRE:

WHERE WATCHED:

DATE SEEN:

WHO WITH:

OVERALL SCORE:
☆ ☆ ☆ ☆ ☆

DIRECTOR:
☆ ☆ ☆ ☆ ☆

CAST:
☆ ☆ ☆ ☆ ☆

SCREENPLAY:
☆ ☆ ☆ ☆ ☆

CINEMATOGRAPHY:
☆ ☆ ☆ ☆ ☆

SPECIAL EFFECTS/ANIMATION:
☆ ☆ ☆ ☆ ☆

PRODUCTION DESIGN:
☆ ☆ ☆ ☆ ☆

MUSICAL SCORE:
☆ ☆ ☆ ☆ ☆

COSTUMING AND PROPS:
☆ ☆ ☆ ☆ ☆

NOTES:

TITLE:

YEAR:

GENRE:

WHERE WATCHED:

DATE SEEN:

WHO WITH:

OVERALL SCORE:
☆ ☆ ☆ ☆ ☆

DIRECTOR:
☆ ☆ ☆ ☆ ☆

CAST:
☆ ☆ ☆ ☆ ☆

SCREENPLAY:
☆ ☆ ☆ ☆ ☆

CINEMATOGRAPHY:
☆ ☆ ☆ ☆ ☆

SPECIAL EFFECTS/ANIMATION:
☆ ☆ ☆ ☆ ☆

PRODUCTION DESIGN:
☆ ☆ ☆ ☆ ☆

MUSICAL SCORE:
☆ ☆ ☆ ☆ ☆

COSTUMING AND PROPS:
☆ ☆ ☆ ☆ ☆

NOTES:

TITLE:

YEAR:

GENRE:

WHERE WATCHED: **DATE SEEN:**

WHO WITH: **OVERALL SCORE:**
☆ ☆ ☆ ☆ ☆

DIRECTOR: ☆ ☆ ☆ ☆ ☆

CAST: ☆ ☆ ☆ ☆ ☆

SCREENPLAY: ☆ ☆ ☆ ☆ ☆

CINEMATOGRAPHY: ☆ ☆ ☆ ☆ ☆

SPECIAL EFFECTS/ANIMATION: ☆ ☆ ☆ ☆ ☆

PRODUCTION DESIGN: ☆ ☆ ☆ ☆ ☆

MUSICAL SCORE: ☆ ☆ ☆ ☆ ☆

COSTUMING AND PROPS: ☆ ☆ ☆ ☆ ☆

NOTES:

TITLE:

YEAR:

GENRE:

WHERE WATCHED:

DATE SEEN:

WHO WITH:

OVERALL SCORE:
☆☆☆☆☆

DIRECTOR:
☆☆☆☆☆

CAST:
☆☆☆☆☆

SCREENPLAY:
☆☆☆☆☆

CINEMATOGRAPHY:
☆☆☆☆☆

SPECIAL EFFECTS/ANIMATION:
☆☆☆☆☆

PRODUCTION DESIGN:
☆☆☆☆☆

MUSICAL SCORE:
☆☆☆☆☆

COSTUMING AND PROPS:
☆☆☆☆☆

NOTES:

TITLE:

YEAR:

GENRE:

WHERE WATCHED:

DATE SEEN:

WHO WITH:

OVERALL SCORE:
☆ ☆ ☆ ☆ ☆

DIRECTOR:
☆ ☆ ☆ ☆ ☆

CAST:
☆ ☆ ☆ ☆ ☆

SCREENPLAY:
☆ ☆ ☆ ☆ ☆

CINEMATOGRAPHY:
☆ ☆ ☆ ☆ ☆

SPECIAL EFFECTS/ANIMATION:
☆ ☆ ☆ ☆ ☆

PRODUCTION DESIGN:
☆ ☆ ☆ ☆ ☆

MUSICAL SCORE:
☆ ☆ ☆ ☆ ☆

COSTUMING AND PROPS:
☆ ☆ ☆ ☆ ☆

NOTES:

TITLE:

YEAR:

GENRE:

WHERE WATCHED:

DATE SEEN:

WHO WITH:

OVERALL SCORE:
☆ ☆ ☆ ☆ ☆

DIRECTOR:
☆ ☆ ☆ ☆ ☆

CAST:
☆ ☆ ☆ ☆ ☆

SCREENPLAY:
☆ ☆ ☆ ☆ ☆

CINEMATOGRAPHY:
☆ ☆ ☆ ☆ ☆

SPECIAL EFFECTS/ANIMATION:
☆ ☆ ☆ ☆ ☆

PRODUCTION DESIGN:
☆ ☆ ☆ ☆ ☆

MUSICAL SCORE:
☆ ☆ ☆ ☆ ☆

COSTUMING AND PROPS:
☆ ☆ ☆ ☆ ☆

NOTES:

TITLE:

YEAR:

GENRE:

WHERE WATCHED:

DATE SEEN:

WHO WITH:

OVERALL SCORE: ☆☆☆☆☆

DIRECTOR: ☆☆☆☆☆

CAST: ☆☆☆☆☆

SCREENPLAY: ☆☆☆☆☆

CINEMATOGRAPHY: ☆☆☆☆☆

SPECIAL EFFECTS/ANIMATION: ☆☆☆☆☆

PRODUCTION DESIGN: ☆☆☆☆☆

MUSICAL SCORE: ☆☆☆☆☆

COSTUMING AND PROPS: ☆☆☆☆☆

NOTES:

TITLE:

YEAR:

GENRE:

WHERE WATCHED:

DATE SEEN:

WHO WITH:

OVERALL SCORE:
☆ ☆ ☆ ☆ ☆

DIRECTOR:
☆ ☆ ☆ ☆ ☆

CAST:
☆ ☆ ☆ ☆ ☆

SCREENPLAY:
☆ ☆ ☆ ☆ ☆

CINEMATOGRAPHY:
☆ ☆ ☆ ☆ ☆

SPECIAL EFFECTS/ANIMATION:
☆ ☆ ☆ ☆ ☆

PRODUCTION DESIGN:
☆ ☆ ☆ ☆ ☆

MUSICAL SCORE:
☆ ☆ ☆ ☆ ☆

COSTUMING AND PROPS:
☆ ☆ ☆ ☆ ☆

NOTES:

TITLE:

YEAR:

GENRE:

WHERE WATCHED:

DATE SEEN:

WHO WITH:

OVERALL SCORE: ☆☆☆☆☆

DIRECTOR: ☆☆☆☆☆

CAST: ☆☆☆☆☆

SCREENPLAY: ☆☆☆☆☆

CINEMATOGRAPHY: ☆☆☆☆☆

SPECIAL EFFECTS/ANIMATION: ☆☆☆☆☆

PRODUCTION DESIGN: ☆☆☆☆☆

MUSICAL SCORE: ☆☆☆☆☆

COSTUMING AND PROPS: ☆☆☆☆☆

NOTES:

TITLE:

YEAR:

GENRE:

WHERE WATCHED:

DATE SEEN:

WHO WITH:

OVERALL SCORE:
☆ ☆ ☆ ☆ ☆

DIRECTOR:
☆ ☆ ☆ ☆ ☆

CAST:
☆ ☆ ☆ ☆ ☆

SCREENPLAY:
☆ ☆ ☆ ☆ ☆

CINEMATOGRAPHY:
☆ ☆ ☆ ☆ ☆

SPECIAL EFFECTS/ANIMATION:
☆ ☆ ☆ ☆ ☆

PRODUCTION DESIGN:
☆ ☆ ☆ ☆ ☆

MUSICAL SCORE:
☆ ☆ ☆ ☆ ☆

COSTUMING AND PROPS:
☆ ☆ ☆ ☆ ☆

NOTES:

TITLE:

YEAR:

GENRE:

WHERE WATCHED:

DATE SEEN:

WHO WITH:

OVERALL SCORE: ☆ ☆ ☆ ☆ ☆

DIRECTOR: ☆ ☆ ☆ ☆ ☆

CAST: ☆ ☆ ☆ ☆ ☆

SCREENPLAY: ☆ ☆ ☆ ☆ ☆

CINEMATOGRAPHY: ☆ ☆ ☆ ☆ ☆

SPECIAL EFFECTS/ANIMATION: ☆ ☆ ☆ ☆ ☆

PRODUCTION DESIGN: ☆ ☆ ☆ ☆ ☆

MUSICAL SCORE: ☆ ☆ ☆ ☆ ☆

COSTUMING AND PROPS: ☆ ☆ ☆ ☆ ☆

NOTES:

TITLE:

YEAR:

GENRE:

WHERE WATCHED:

DATE SEEN:

WHO WITH:

OVERALL SCORE:
☆ ☆ ☆ ☆ ☆

DIRECTOR:
☆ ☆ ☆ ☆ ☆

CAST:
☆ ☆ ☆ ☆ ☆

SCREENPLAY:
☆ ☆ ☆ ☆ ☆

CINEMATOGRAPHY:
☆ ☆ ☆ ☆ ☆

SPECIAL EFFECTS/ANIMATION:
☆ ☆ ☆ ☆ ☆

PRODUCTION DESIGN:
☆ ☆ ☆ ☆ ☆

MUSICAL SCORE:
☆ ☆ ☆ ☆ ☆

COSTUMING AND PROPS:
☆ ☆ ☆ ☆ ☆

NOTES:

TITLE:

YEAR:

GENRE:

WHERE WATCHED:

DATE SEEN:

WHO WITH:

OVERALL SCORE:
☆ ☆ ☆ ☆ ☆

DIRECTOR:
☆ ☆ ☆ ☆ ☆

CAST:
☆ ☆ ☆ ☆ ☆

SCREENPLAY:
☆ ☆ ☆ ☆ ☆

CINEMATOGRAPHY:
☆ ☆ ☆ ☆ ☆

SPECIAL EFFECTS/ANIMATION:
☆ ☆ ☆ ☆ ☆

PRODUCTION DESIGN:
☆ ☆ ☆ ☆ ☆

MUSICAL SCORE:
☆ ☆ ☆ ☆ ☆

COSTUMING AND PROPS:
☆ ☆ ☆ ☆ ☆

NOTES:

TITLE:

YEAR:

GENRE:

WHERE WATCHED:

DATE SEEN:

WHO WITH:

OVERALL SCORE:
☆ ☆ ☆ ☆ ☆

DIRECTOR:
☆ ☆ ☆ ☆ ☆

CAST:
☆ ☆ ☆ ☆ ☆

SCREENPLAY:
☆ ☆ ☆ ☆ ☆

CINEMATOGRAPHY:
☆ ☆ ☆ ☆ ☆

SPECIAL EFFECTS/ANIMATION:
☆ ☆ ☆ ☆ ☆

PRODUCTION DESIGN:
☆ ☆ ☆ ☆ ☆

MUSICAL SCORE:
☆ ☆ ☆ ☆ ☆

COSTUMING AND PROPS:
☆ ☆ ☆ ☆ ☆

NOTES:

TITLE: **YEAR:**

GENRE:

WHERE WATCHED: **DATE SEEN:**

WHO WITH: **OVERALL SCORE:**
☆ ☆ ☆ ☆ ☆

DIRECTOR: ☆ ☆ ☆ ☆ ☆

CAST: ☆ ☆ ☆ ☆ ☆

SCREENPLAY: ☆ ☆ ☆ ☆ ☆

CINEMATOGRAPHY: ☆ ☆ ☆ ☆ ☆

SPECIAL EFFECTS/ANIMATION: ☆ ☆ ☆ ☆ ☆

PRODUCTION DESIGN: ☆ ☆ ☆ ☆ ☆

MUSICAL SCORE: ☆ ☆ ☆ ☆ ☆

COSTUMING AND PROPS: ☆ ☆ ☆ ☆ ☆

NOTES:

TITLE:

YEAR:

GENRE:

WHERE WATCHED:

DATE SEEN:

WHO WITH:

OVERALL SCORE:

☆ ☆ ☆ ☆ ☆

DIRECTOR:

☆ ☆ ☆ ☆ ☆

CAST:

☆ ☆ ☆ ☆ ☆

SCREENPLAY:

☆ ☆ ☆ ☆ ☆

CINEMATOGRAPHY:

☆ ☆ ☆ ☆ ☆

SPECIAL EFFECTS/ANIMATION:

☆ ☆ ☆ ☆ ☆

PRODUCTION DESIGN:

☆ ☆ ☆ ☆ ☆

MUSICAL SCORE:

☆ ☆ ☆ ☆ ☆

COSTUMING AND PROPS:

☆ ☆ ☆ ☆ ☆

NOTES:

TITLE:

YEAR:

GENRE:

WHERE WATCHED:

DATE SEEN:

WHO WITH:

OVERALL SCORE:
☆ ☆ ☆ ☆ ☆

DIRECTOR:
☆ ☆ ☆ ☆ ☆

CAST:
☆ ☆ ☆ ☆ ☆

SCREENPLAY:
☆ ☆ ☆ ☆ ☆

CINEMATOGRAPHY:
☆ ☆ ☆ ☆ ☆

SPECIAL EFFECTS/ANIMATION:
☆ ☆ ☆ ☆ ☆

PRODUCTION DESIGN:
☆ ☆ ☆ ☆ ☆

MUSICAL SCORE:
☆ ☆ ☆ ☆ ☆

COSTUMING AND PROPS:
☆ ☆ ☆ ☆ ☆

NOTES:

TITLE:

YEAR:

GENRE:

WHERE WATCHED:

DATE SEEN:

WHO WITH:

OVERALL SCORE:
☆ ☆ ☆ ☆ ☆

DIRECTOR:
☆ ☆ ☆ ☆ ☆

CAST:
☆ ☆ ☆ ☆ ☆

SCREENPLAY:
☆ ☆ ☆ ☆ ☆

CINEMATOGRAPHY:
☆ ☆ ☆ ☆ ☆

SPECIAL EFFECTS/ANIMATION:
☆ ☆ ☆ ☆ ☆

PRODUCTION DESIGN:
☆ ☆ ☆ ☆ ☆

MUSICAL SCORE:
☆ ☆ ☆ ☆ ☆

COSTUMING AND PROPS:
☆ ☆ ☆ ☆ ☆

NOTES:

TITLE:

YEAR:

GENRE:

WHERE WATCHED:

DATE SEEN:

WHO WITH:

OVERALL SCORE:
☆ ☆ ☆ ☆ ☆

DIRECTOR:
☆ ☆ ☆ ☆ ☆

CAST:
☆ ☆ ☆ ☆ ☆

SCREENPLAY:
☆ ☆ ☆ ☆ ☆

CINEMATOGRAPHY:
☆ ☆ ☆ ☆ ☆

SPECIAL EFFECTS/ANIMATION:
☆ ☆ ☆ ☆ ☆

PRODUCTION DESIGN:
☆ ☆ ☆ ☆ ☆

MUSICAL SCORE:
☆ ☆ ☆ ☆ ☆

COSTUMING AND PROPS:
☆ ☆ ☆ ☆ ☆

NOTES:

TITLE:

YEAR:

GENRE:

WHERE WATCHED:

DATE SEEN:

WHO WITH:

OVERALL SCORE:

☆ ☆ ☆ ☆ ☆

DIRECTOR:

☆ ☆ ☆ ☆ ☆

CAST:

☆ ☆ ☆ ☆ ☆

SCREENPLAY:

☆ ☆ ☆ ☆ ☆

CINEMATOGRAPHY:

☆ ☆ ☆ ☆ ☆

SPECIAL EFFECTS/ANIMATION:

☆ ☆ ☆ ☆ ☆

PRODUCTION DESIGN:

☆ ☆ ☆ ☆ ☆

MUSICAL SCORE:

☆ ☆ ☆ ☆ ☆

COSTUMING AND PROPS:

☆ ☆ ☆ ☆ ☆

NOTES:

TITLE:

YEAR:

GENRE:

WHERE WATCHED:

DATE SEEN:

WHO WITH:

OVERALL SCORE:
☆☆☆☆☆

DIRECTOR:
☆☆☆☆☆

CAST:
☆☆☆☆☆

SCREENPLAY:
☆☆☆☆☆

CINEMATOGRAPHY:
☆☆☆☆☆

SPECIAL EFFECTS/ANIMATION:
☆☆☆☆☆

PRODUCTION DESIGN:
☆☆☆☆☆

MUSICAL SCORE:
☆☆☆☆☆

COSTUMING AND PROPS:
☆☆☆☆☆

NOTES:

TITLE:

YEAR:

GENRE:

WHERE WATCHED:

DATE SEEN:

WHO WITH:

OVERALL SCORE: ☆ ☆ ☆ ☆ ☆

DIRECTOR: ☆ ☆ ☆ ☆ ☆

CAST: ☆ ☆ ☆ ☆ ☆

SCREENPLAY: ☆ ☆ ☆ ☆ ☆

CINEMATOGRAPHY: ☆ ☆ ☆ ☆ ☆

SPECIAL EFFECTS/ANIMATION: ☆ ☆ ☆ ☆ ☆

PRODUCTION DESIGN: ☆ ☆ ☆ ☆ ☆

MUSICAL SCORE: ☆ ☆ ☆ ☆ ☆

COSTUMING AND PROPS: ☆ ☆ ☆ ☆ ☆

NOTES:

TITLE:

YEAR:

GENRE:

WHERE WATCHED:

DATE SEEN:

WHO WITH:

OVERALL SCORE: ☆☆☆☆☆

DIRECTOR: ☆☆☆☆☆

CAST: ☆☆☆☆☆

SCREENPLAY: ☆☆☆☆☆

CINEMATOGRAPHY: ☆☆☆☆☆

SPECIAL EFFECTS/ANIMATION: ☆☆☆☆☆

PRODUCTION DESIGN: ☆☆☆☆☆

MUSICAL SCORE: ☆☆☆☆☆

COSTUMING AND PROPS: ☆☆☆☆☆

NOTES:

TITLE:

YEAR:

GENRE:

WHERE WATCHED:

DATE SEEN:

WHO WITH:

OVERALL SCORE:
☆ ☆ ☆ ☆ ☆

DIRECTOR:
☆ ☆ ☆ ☆ ☆

CAST:
☆ ☆ ☆ ☆ ☆

SCREENPLAY:
☆ ☆ ☆ ☆ ☆

CINEMATOGRAPHY:
☆ ☆ ☆ ☆ ☆

SPECIAL EFFECTS/ANIMATION:
☆ ☆ ☆ ☆ ☆

PRODUCTION DESIGN:
☆ ☆ ☆ ☆ ☆

MUSICAL SCORE:
☆ ☆ ☆ ☆ ☆

COSTUMING AND PROPS:
☆ ☆ ☆ ☆ ☆

NOTES:

TITLE:

YEAR:

GENRE:

WHERE WATCHED:

DATE SEEN:

WHO WITH:

OVERALL SCORE: ☆☆☆☆☆

DIRECTOR: ☆☆☆☆☆

CAST: ☆☆☆☆☆

SCREENPLAY: ☆☆☆☆☆

CINEMATOGRAPHY: ☆☆☆☆☆

SPECIAL EFFECTS/ANIMATION: ☆☆☆☆☆

PRODUCTION DESIGN: ☆☆☆☆☆

MUSICAL SCORE: ☆☆☆☆☆

COSTUMING AND PROPS: ☆☆☆☆☆

NOTES:

TITLE:

WHERE WATCHED:

WHO WITH:

YEAR:

GENRE:

DATE SEEN:

OVERALL SCORE:
☆ ☆ ☆ ☆ ☆

DIRECTOR:
☆ ☆ ☆ ☆ ☆

CAST:
☆ ☆ ☆ ☆ ☆

SCREENPLAY:
☆ ☆ ☆ ☆ ☆

CINEMATOGRAPHY:
☆ ☆ ☆ ☆ ☆

SPECIAL EFFECTS/ANIMATION:
☆ ☆ ☆ ☆ ☆

PRODUCTION DESIGN:
☆ ☆ ☆ ☆ ☆

MUSICAL SCORE:
☆ ☆ ☆ ☆ ☆

COSTUMING AND PROPS:
☆ ☆ ☆ ☆ ☆

NOTES:

TITLE:

YEAR:

GENRE:

WHERE WATCHED:

DATE SEEN:

WHO WITH:

OVERALL SCORE: ☆ ☆ ☆ ☆ ☆

DIRECTOR: ☆ ☆ ☆ ☆ ☆

CAST: ☆ ☆ ☆ ☆ ☆

SCREENPLAY: ☆ ☆ ☆ ☆ ☆

CINEMATOGRAPHY: ☆ ☆ ☆ ☆ ☆

SPECIAL EFFECTS/ANIMATION: ☆ ☆ ☆ ☆ ☆

PRODUCTION DESIGN: ☆ ☆ ☆ ☆ ☆

MUSICAL SCORE: ☆ ☆ ☆ ☆ ☆

COSTUMING AND PROPS: ☆ ☆ ☆ ☆ ☆

NOTES:

TITLE:

YEAR:

GENRE:

WHERE WATCHED:

DATE SEEN:

WHO WITH:

OVERALL SCORE:
☆ ☆ ☆ ☆ ☆

DIRECTOR:
☆ ☆ ☆ ☆ ☆

CAST:
☆ ☆ ☆ ☆ ☆

SCREENPLAY:
☆ ☆ ☆ ☆ ☆

CINEMATOGRAPHY:
☆ ☆ ☆ ☆ ☆

SPECIAL EFFECTS/ANIMATION:
☆ ☆ ☆ ☆ ☆

PRODUCTION DESIGN:
☆ ☆ ☆ ☆ ☆

MUSICAL SCORE:
☆ ☆ ☆ ☆ ☆

COSTUMING AND PROPS:
☆ ☆ ☆ ☆ ☆

NOTES:

TITLE:

YEAR:

GENRE:

WHERE WATCHED:

DATE SEEN:

WHO WITH:

OVERALL SCORE: ☆ ☆ ☆ ☆ ☆

DIRECTOR: ☆ ☆ ☆ ☆ ☆

CAST: ☆ ☆ ☆ ☆ ☆

SCREENPLAY: ☆ ☆ ☆ ☆ ☆

CINEMATOGRAPHY: ☆ ☆ ☆ ☆ ☆

SPECIAL EFFECTS/ANIMATION: ☆ ☆ ☆ ☆ ☆

PRODUCTION DESIGN: ☆ ☆ ☆ ☆ ☆

MUSICAL SCORE: ☆ ☆ ☆ ☆ ☆

COSTUMING AND PROPS: ☆ ☆ ☆ ☆ ☆

NOTES:

TITLE:

YEAR:

GENRE:

WHERE WATCHED:

DATE SEEN:

WHO WITH:

OVERALL SCORE:
☆ ☆ ☆ ☆ ☆

DIRECTOR:
☆ ☆ ☆ ☆ ☆

CAST:
☆ ☆ ☆ ☆ ☆

SCREENPLAY:
☆ ☆ ☆ ☆ ☆

CINEMATOGRAPHY:
☆ ☆ ☆ ☆ ☆

SPECIAL EFFECTS/ANIMATION:
☆ ☆ ☆ ☆ ☆

PRODUCTION DESIGN:
☆ ☆ ☆ ☆ ☆

MUSICAL SCORE:
☆ ☆ ☆ ☆ ☆

COSTUMING AND PROPS:
☆ ☆ ☆ ☆ ☆

NOTES:

TITLE:

YEAR:

GENRE:

WHERE WATCHED:

DATE SEEN:

WHO WITH:

OVERALL SCORE:
☆ ☆ ☆ ☆ ☆

DIRECTOR:
☆ ☆ ☆ ☆ ☆

CAST:
☆ ☆ ☆ ☆ ☆

SCREENPLAY:
☆ ☆ ☆ ☆ ☆

CINEMATOGRAPHY:
☆ ☆ ☆ ☆ ☆

SPECIAL EFFECTS/ANIMATION:
☆ ☆ ☆ ☆ ☆

PRODUCTION DESIGN:
☆ ☆ ☆ ☆ ☆

MUSICAL SCORE:
☆ ☆ ☆ ☆ ☆

COSTUMING AND PROPS:
☆ ☆ ☆ ☆ ☆

NOTES:

TITLE:

YEAR:

GENRE:

WHERE WATCHED:

DATE SEEN:

WHO WITH:

OVERALL SCORE: ☆☆☆☆☆

DIRECTOR: ☆☆☆☆☆

CAST: ☆☆☆☆☆

SCREENPLAY: ☆☆☆☆☆

CINEMATOGRAPHY: ☆☆☆☆☆

SPECIAL EFFECTS/ANIMATION: ☆☆☆☆☆

PRODUCTION DESIGN: ☆☆☆☆☆

MUSICAL SCORE: ☆☆☆☆☆

COSTUMING AND PROPS: ☆☆☆☆☆

NOTES:

TITLE:

YEAR:

GENRE:

WHERE WATCHED:

DATE SEEN:

WHO WITH:

OVERALL SCORE:
☆ ☆ ☆ ☆ ☆

DIRECTOR:
☆ ☆ ☆ ☆ ☆

CAST:
☆ ☆ ☆ ☆ ☆

SCREENPLAY:
☆ ☆ ☆ ☆ ☆

CINEMATOGRAPHY:
☆ ☆ ☆ ☆ ☆

SPECIAL EFFECTS/ANIMATION:
☆ ☆ ☆ ☆ ☆

PRODUCTION DESIGN:
☆ ☆ ☆ ☆ ☆

MUSICAL SCORE:
☆ ☆ ☆ ☆ ☆

COSTUMING AND PROPS:
☆ ☆ ☆ ☆ ☆

NOTES:

TITLE:

YEAR:

GENRE:

WHERE WATCHED:

DATE SEEN:

WHO WITH:

OVERALL SCORE:
☆☆☆☆☆

DIRECTOR:
☆☆☆☆☆

CAST:
☆☆☆☆☆

SCREENPLAY:
☆☆☆☆☆

CINEMATOGRAPHY:
☆☆☆☆☆

SPECIAL EFFECTS/ANIMATION:
☆☆☆☆☆

PRODUCTION DESIGN:
☆☆☆☆☆

MUSICAL SCORE:
☆☆☆☆☆

COSTUMING AND PROPS:
☆☆☆☆☆

NOTES:

TITLE:

YEAR:

GENRE:

WHERE WATCHED:

DATE SEEN:

WHO WITH:

OVERALL SCORE:

☆ ☆ ☆ ☆ ☆

DIRECTOR:

☆ ☆ ☆ ☆ ☆

CAST:

☆ ☆ ☆ ☆ ☆

SCREENPLAY:

☆ ☆ ☆ ☆ ☆

CINEMATOGRAPHY:

☆ ☆ ☆ ☆ ☆

SPECIAL EFFECTS/ANIMATION:

☆ ☆ ☆ ☆ ☆

PRODUCTION DESIGN:

☆ ☆ ☆ ☆ ☆

MUSICAL SCORE:

☆ ☆ ☆ ☆ ☆

COSTUMING AND PROPS:

☆ ☆ ☆ ☆ ☆

NOTES:

TITLE:

YEAR:

GENRE:

WHERE WATCHED:

DATE SEEN:

WHO WITH:

OVERALL SCORE: ☆☆☆☆☆

DIRECTOR: ☆☆☆☆☆

CAST: ☆☆☆☆☆

SCREENPLAY: ☆☆☆☆☆

CINEMATOGRAPHY: ☆☆☆☆☆

SPECIAL EFFECTS/ANIMATION: ☆☆☆☆☆

PRODUCTION DESIGN: ☆☆☆☆☆

MUSICAL SCORE: ☆☆☆☆☆

COSTUMING AND PROPS: ☆☆☆☆☆

NOTES:

TITLE:

YEAR:

GENRE:

WHERE WATCHED:

DATE SEEN:

WHO WITH:

OVERALL SCORE:
☆ ☆ ☆ ☆ ☆

DIRECTOR:
☆ ☆ ☆ ☆ ☆

CAST:
☆ ☆ ☆ ☆ ☆

SCREENPLAY:
☆ ☆ ☆ ☆ ☆

CINEMATOGRAPHY:
☆ ☆ ☆ ☆ ☆

SPECIAL EFFECTS/ANIMATION:
☆ ☆ ☆ ☆ ☆

PRODUCTION DESIGN:
☆ ☆ ☆ ☆ ☆

MUSICAL SCORE:
☆ ☆ ☆ ☆ ☆

COSTUMING AND PROPS:
☆ ☆ ☆ ☆ ☆

NOTES:

TITLE:

YEAR:

GENRE:

WHERE WATCHED:

DATE SEEN:

WHO WITH:

OVERALL SCORE: ☆☆☆☆☆

DIRECTOR: ☆☆☆☆☆

CAST: ☆☆☆☆☆

SCREENPLAY: ☆☆☆☆☆

CINEMATOGRAPHY: ☆☆☆☆☆

SPECIAL EFFECTS/ANIMATION: ☆☆☆☆☆

PRODUCTION DESIGN: ☆☆☆☆☆

MUSICAL SCORE: ☆☆☆☆☆

COSTUMING AND PROPS: ☆☆☆☆☆

NOTES:

TITLE:

YEAR:

GENRE:

WHERE WATCHED:

DATE SEEN:

WHO WITH:

OVERALL SCORE: ☆ ☆ ☆ ☆ ☆

DIRECTOR: ☆ ☆ ☆ ☆ ☆

CAST: ☆ ☆ ☆ ☆ ☆

SCREENPLAY: ☆ ☆ ☆ ☆ ☆

CINEMATOGRAPHY: ☆ ☆ ☆ ☆ ☆

SPECIAL EFFECTS/ANIMATION: ☆ ☆ ☆ ☆ ☆

PRODUCTION DESIGN: ☆ ☆ ☆ ☆ ☆

MUSICAL SCORE: ☆ ☆ ☆ ☆ ☆

COSTUMING AND PROPS: ☆ ☆ ☆ ☆ ☆

NOTES:

TITLE:

YEAR:

GENRE:

WHERE WATCHED:

DATE SEEN:

WHO WITH:

OVERALL SCORE:
☆☆☆☆☆

DIRECTOR:
☆☆☆☆☆

CAST:
☆☆☆☆☆

SCREENPLAY:
☆☆☆☆☆

CINEMATOGRAPHY:
☆☆☆☆☆

SPECIAL EFFECTS/ANIMATION:
☆☆☆☆☆

PRODUCTION DESIGN:
☆☆☆☆☆

MUSICAL SCORE:
☆☆☆☆☆

COSTUMING AND PROPS:
☆☆☆☆☆

NOTES:

TITLE:

YEAR:

GENRE:

WHERE WATCHED:

DATE SEEN:

WHO WITH:

OVERALL SCORE:
☆ ☆ ☆ ☆ ☆

DIRECTOR:
☆ ☆ ☆ ☆ ☆

CAST:
☆ ☆ ☆ ☆ ☆

SCREENPLAY:
☆ ☆ ☆ ☆ ☆

CINEMATOGRAPHY:
☆ ☆ ☆ ☆ ☆

SPECIAL EFFECTS/ANIMATION:
☆ ☆ ☆ ☆ ☆

PRODUCTION DESIGN:
☆ ☆ ☆ ☆ ☆

MUSICAL SCORE:
☆ ☆ ☆ ☆ ☆

COSTUMING AND PROPS:
☆ ☆ ☆ ☆ ☆

NOTES:

TITLE:

YEAR:

GENRE:

WHERE WATCHED:

DATE SEEN:

WHO WITH:

OVERALL SCORE:
☆ ☆ ☆ ☆ ☆

DIRECTOR:
☆ ☆ ☆ ☆ ☆

CAST:
☆ ☆ ☆ ☆ ☆

SCREENPLAY:
☆ ☆ ☆ ☆ ☆

CINEMATOGRAPHY:
☆ ☆ ☆ ☆ ☆

SPECIAL EFFECTS/ANIMATION:
☆ ☆ ☆ ☆ ☆

PRODUCTION DESIGN:
☆ ☆ ☆ ☆ ☆

MUSICAL SCORE:
☆ ☆ ☆ ☆ ☆

COSTUMING AND PROPS:
☆ ☆ ☆ ☆ ☆

NOTES:

TITLE:

YEAR:

GENRE:

WHERE WATCHED:

DATE SEEN:

WHO WITH:

OVERALL SCORE:
☆ ☆ ☆ ☆ ☆

DIRECTOR:
☆ ☆ ☆ ☆ ☆

CAST:
☆ ☆ ☆ ☆ ☆

SCREENPLAY:
☆ ☆ ☆ ☆ ☆

CINEMATOGRAPHY:
☆ ☆ ☆ ☆ ☆

SPECIAL EFFECTS/ANIMATION:
☆ ☆ ☆ ☆ ☆

PRODUCTION DESIGN:
☆ ☆ ☆ ☆ ☆

MUSICAL SCORE:
☆ ☆ ☆ ☆ ☆

COSTUMING AND PROPS:
☆ ☆ ☆ ☆ ☆

NOTES:

TITLE:

YEAR:

GENRE:

WHERE WATCHED:

DATE SEEN:

WHO WITH:

OVERALL SCORE: ☆☆☆☆☆

DIRECTOR: ☆☆☆☆☆

CAST: ☆☆☆☆☆

SCREENPLAY: ☆☆☆☆☆

CINEMATOGRAPHY: ☆☆☆☆☆

SPECIAL EFFECTS/ANIMATION: ☆☆☆☆☆

PRODUCTION DESIGN: ☆☆☆☆☆

MUSICAL SCORE: ☆☆☆☆☆

COSTUMING AND PROPS: ☆☆☆☆☆

NOTES:

TITLE:

YEAR:

GENRE:

WHERE WATCHED:

DATE SEEN:

WHO WITH:

OVERALL SCORE:
☆ ☆ ☆ ☆ ☆

DIRECTOR:
☆ ☆ ☆ ☆ ☆

CAST:
☆ ☆ ☆ ☆ ☆

SCREENPLAY:
☆ ☆ ☆ ☆ ☆

CINEMATOGRAPHY:
☆ ☆ ☆ ☆ ☆

SPECIAL EFFECTS/ANIMATION:
☆ ☆ ☆ ☆ ☆

PRODUCTION DESIGN:
☆ ☆ ☆ ☆ ☆

MUSICAL SCORE:
☆ ☆ ☆ ☆ ☆

COSTUMING AND PROPS:
☆ ☆ ☆ ☆ ☆

NOTES:

TITLE:

YEAR:

GENRE:

WHERE WATCHED:

DATE SEEN:

WHO WITH:

OVERALL SCORE:
☆ ☆ ☆ ☆ ☆

DIRECTOR:
☆ ☆ ☆ ☆ ☆

CAST:
☆ ☆ ☆ ☆ ☆

SCREENPLAY:
☆ ☆ ☆ ☆ ☆

CINEMATOGRAPHY:
☆ ☆ ☆ ☆ ☆

SPECIAL EFFECTS/ANIMATION:
☆ ☆ ☆ ☆ ☆

PRODUCTION DESIGN:
☆ ☆ ☆ ☆ ☆

MUSICAL SCORE:
☆ ☆ ☆ ☆ ☆

COSTUMING AND PROPS:
☆ ☆ ☆ ☆ ☆

NOTES:

TITLE:

YEAR:

GENRE:

WHERE WATCHED:

DATE SEEN:

WHO WITH:

OVERALL SCORE:

☆ ☆ ☆ ☆ ☆

DIRECTOR:

☆ ☆ ☆ ☆ ☆

CAST:

☆ ☆ ☆ ☆ ☆

SCREENPLAY:

☆ ☆ ☆ ☆ ☆

CINEMATOGRAPHY:

☆ ☆ ☆ ☆ ☆

SPECIAL EFFECTS/ANIMATION:

☆ ☆ ☆ ☆ ☆

PRODUCTION DESIGN:

☆ ☆ ☆ ☆ ☆

MUSICAL SCORE:

☆ ☆ ☆ ☆ ☆

COSTUMING AND PROPS:

☆ ☆ ☆ ☆ ☆

NOTES:

TITLE:

YEAR:

GENRE:

WHERE WATCHED:

DATE SEEN:

WHO WITH:

OVERALL SCORE:
☆☆☆☆☆

DIRECTOR:
☆☆☆☆☆

CAST:
☆☆☆☆☆

SCREENPLAY:
☆☆☆☆☆

CINEMATOGRAPHY:
☆☆☆☆☆

SPECIAL EFFECTS/ANIMATION:
☆☆☆☆☆

PRODUCTION DESIGN:
☆☆☆☆☆

MUSICAL SCORE:
☆☆☆☆☆

COSTUMING AND PROPS:
☆☆☆☆☆

NOTES:

TITLE:

YEAR:

GENRE:

WHERE WATCHED:

DATE SEEN:

WHO WITH:

OVERALL SCORE:
☆ ☆ ☆ ☆ ☆

DIRECTOR:
☆ ☆ ☆ ☆ ☆

CAST:
☆ ☆ ☆ ☆ ☆

SCREENPLAY:
☆ ☆ ☆ ☆ ☆

CINEMATOGRAPHY:
☆ ☆ ☆ ☆ ☆

SPECIAL EFFECTS/ANIMATION:
☆ ☆ ☆ ☆ ☆

PRODUCTION DESIGN:
☆ ☆ ☆ ☆ ☆

MUSICAL SCORE:
☆ ☆ ☆ ☆ ☆

COSTUMING AND PROPS:
☆ ☆ ☆ ☆ ☆

NOTES:

TITLE:

YEAR:

GENRE:

WHERE WATCHED:

DATE SEEN:

WHO WITH:

OVERALL SCORE:
☆ ☆ ☆ ☆ ☆

DIRECTOR:
☆ ☆ ☆ ☆ ☆

CAST:
☆ ☆ ☆ ☆ ☆

SCREENPLAY:
☆ ☆ ☆ ☆ ☆

CINEMATOGRAPHY:
☆ ☆ ☆ ☆ ☆

SPECIAL EFFECTS/ANIMATION:
☆ ☆ ☆ ☆ ☆

PRODUCTION DESIGN:
☆ ☆ ☆ ☆ ☆

MUSICAL SCORE:
☆ ☆ ☆ ☆ ☆

COSTUMING AND PROPS:
☆ ☆ ☆ ☆ ☆

NOTES:

TITLE:

YEAR:

GENRE:

WHERE WATCHED:

DATE SEEN:

WHO WITH:

OVERALL SCORE:

☆ ☆ ☆ ☆ ☆

DIRECTOR:

☆ ☆ ☆ ☆ ☆

CAST:

☆ ☆ ☆ ☆ ☆

SCREENPLAY:

☆ ☆ ☆ ☆ ☆

CINEMATOGRAPHY:

☆ ☆ ☆ ☆ ☆

SPECIAL EFFECTS/ANIMATION:

☆ ☆ ☆ ☆ ☆

PRODUCTION DESIGN:

☆ ☆ ☆ ☆ ☆

MUSICAL SCORE:

☆ ☆ ☆ ☆ ☆

COSTUMING AND PROPS:

☆ ☆ ☆ ☆ ☆

NOTES:

TITLE:

YEAR:

GENRE:

WHERE WATCHED:

DATE SEEN:

WHO WITH:

OVERALL SCORE:
☆ ☆ ☆ ☆ ☆

DIRECTOR:
☆ ☆ ☆ ☆ ☆

CAST:
☆ ☆ ☆ ☆ ☆

SCREENPLAY:
☆ ☆ ☆ ☆ ☆

CINEMATOGRAPHY:
☆ ☆ ☆ ☆ ☆

SPECIAL EFFECTS/ANIMATION:
☆ ☆ ☆ ☆ ☆

PRODUCTION DESIGN:
☆ ☆ ☆ ☆ ☆

MUSICAL SCORE:
☆ ☆ ☆ ☆ ☆

COSTUMING AND PROPS:
☆ ☆ ☆ ☆ ☆

NOTES:

TITLE:

YEAR:

GENRE:

WHERE WATCHED:

DATE SEEN:

WHO WITH:

OVERALL SCORE:
☆ ☆ ☆ ☆ ☆

DIRECTOR:
☆ ☆ ☆ ☆ ☆

CAST:
☆ ☆ ☆ ☆ ☆

SCREENPLAY:
☆ ☆ ☆ ☆ ☆

CINEMATOGRAPHY:
☆ ☆ ☆ ☆ ☆

SPECIAL EFFECTS/ANIMATION:
☆ ☆ ☆ ☆ ☆

PRODUCTION DESIGN:
☆ ☆ ☆ ☆ ☆

MUSICAL SCORE:
☆ ☆ ☆ ☆ ☆

COSTUMING AND PROPS:
☆ ☆ ☆ ☆ ☆

NOTES:

TITLE:

YEAR:

GENRE:

WHERE WATCHED:

DATE SEEN:

WHO WITH:

OVERALL SCORE:
☆ ☆ ☆ ☆ ☆

DIRECTOR:
☆ ☆ ☆ ☆ ☆

CAST:
☆ ☆ ☆ ☆ ☆

SCREENPLAY:
☆ ☆ ☆ ☆ ☆

CINEMATOGRAPHY:
☆ ☆ ☆ ☆ ☆

SPECIAL EFFECTS/ANIMATION:
☆ ☆ ☆ ☆ ☆

PRODUCTION DESIGN:
☆ ☆ ☆ ☆ ☆

MUSICAL SCORE:
☆ ☆ ☆ ☆ ☆

COSTUMING AND PROPS:
☆ ☆ ☆ ☆ ☆

NOTES:

TITLE:

YEAR:

GENRE:

WHERE WATCHED:

DATE SEEN:

WHO WITH:

OVERALL SCORE:
☆ ☆ ☆ ☆ ☆

DIRECTOR:
☆ ☆ ☆ ☆ ☆

CAST:
☆ ☆ ☆ ☆ ☆

SCREENPLAY:
☆ ☆ ☆ ☆ ☆

CINEMATOGRAPHY:
☆ ☆ ☆ ☆ ☆

SPECIAL EFFECTS/ANIMATION:
☆ ☆ ☆ ☆ ☆

PRODUCTION DESIGN:
☆ ☆ ☆ ☆ ☆

MUSICAL SCORE:
☆ ☆ ☆ ☆ ☆

COSTUMING AND PROPS:
☆ ☆ ☆ ☆ ☆

NOTES:

TITLE:

YEAR:

GENRE:

WHERE WATCHED:

DATE SEEN:

WHO WITH:

OVERALL SCORE: ☆ ☆ ☆ ☆ ☆

DIRECTOR: ☆ ☆ ☆ ☆ ☆

CAST: ☆ ☆ ☆ ☆ ☆

SCREENPLAY: ☆ ☆ ☆ ☆ ☆

CINEMATOGRAPHY: ☆ ☆ ☆ ☆ ☆

SPECIAL EFFECTS/ANIMATION: ☆ ☆ ☆ ☆ ☆

PRODUCTION DESIGN: ☆ ☆ ☆ ☆ ☆

MUSICAL SCORE: ☆ ☆ ☆ ☆ ☆

COSTUMING AND PROPS: ☆ ☆ ☆ ☆ ☆

NOTES:

TITLE:

YEAR:

GENRE:

WHERE WATCHED:

DATE SEEN:

WHO WITH:

OVERALL SCORE:
☆ ☆ ☆ ☆ ☆

DIRECTOR:
☆ ☆ ☆ ☆ ☆

CAST:
☆ ☆ ☆ ☆ ☆

SCREENPLAY:
☆ ☆ ☆ ☆ ☆

CINEMATOGRAPHY:
☆ ☆ ☆ ☆ ☆

SPECIAL EFFECTS/ANIMATION:
☆ ☆ ☆ ☆ ☆

PRODUCTION DESIGN:
☆ ☆ ☆ ☆ ☆

MUSICAL SCORE:
☆ ☆ ☆ ☆ ☆

COSTUMING AND PROPS:
☆ ☆ ☆ ☆ ☆

NOTES:

TITLE:

YEAR:

GENRE:

WHERE WATCHED:

DATE SEEN:

WHO WITH:

OVERALL SCORE: ☆ ☆ ☆ ☆ ☆

DIRECTOR: ☆ ☆ ☆ ☆ ☆

CAST: ☆ ☆ ☆ ☆ ☆

SCREENPLAY: ☆ ☆ ☆ ☆ ☆

CINEMATOGRAPHY: ☆ ☆ ☆ ☆ ☆

SPECIAL EFFECTS/ANIMATION: ☆ ☆ ☆ ☆ ☆

PRODUCTION DESIGN: ☆ ☆ ☆ ☆ ☆

MUSICAL SCORE: ☆ ☆ ☆ ☆ ☆

COSTUMING AND PROPS: ☆ ☆ ☆ ☆ ☆

NOTES:

TITLE:

YEAR:

GENRE:

WHERE WATCHED:

DATE SEEN:

WHO WITH:

OVERALL SCORE:
☆ ☆ ☆ ☆ ☆

DIRECTOR:
☆ ☆ ☆ ☆ ☆

CAST:
☆ ☆ ☆ ☆ ☆

SCREENPLAY:
☆ ☆ ☆ ☆ ☆

CINEMATOGRAPHY:
☆ ☆ ☆ ☆ ☆

SPECIAL EFFECTS/ANIMATION:
☆ ☆ ☆ ☆ ☆

PRODUCTION DESIGN:
☆ ☆ ☆ ☆ ☆

MUSICAL SCORE:
☆ ☆ ☆ ☆ ☆

COSTUMING AND PROPS:
☆ ☆ ☆ ☆ ☆

NOTES:

TITLE:

YEAR:

GENRE:

WHERE WATCHED:

DATE SEEN:

WHO WITH:

OVERALL SCORE:
☆ ☆ ☆ ☆ ☆

DIRECTOR:
☆ ☆ ☆ ☆ ☆

CAST:
☆ ☆ ☆ ☆ ☆

SCREENPLAY:
☆ ☆ ☆ ☆ ☆

CINEMATOGRAPHY:
☆ ☆ ☆ ☆ ☆

SPECIAL EFFECTS/ANIMATION:
☆ ☆ ☆ ☆ ☆

PRODUCTION DESIGN:
☆ ☆ ☆ ☆ ☆

MUSICAL SCORE:
☆ ☆ ☆ ☆ ☆

COSTUMING AND PROPS:
☆ ☆ ☆ ☆ ☆

NOTES:

TITLE:

YEAR:

GENRE:

WHERE WATCHED:

DATE SEEN:

WHO WITH:

OVERALL SCORE:
☆ ☆ ☆ ☆ ☆

DIRECTOR:
☆ ☆ ☆ ☆ ☆

CAST:
☆ ☆ ☆ ☆ ☆

SCREENPLAY:
☆ ☆ ☆ ☆ ☆

CINEMATOGRAPHY:
☆ ☆ ☆ ☆ ☆

SPECIAL EFFECTS/ANIMATION:
☆ ☆ ☆ ☆ ☆

PRODUCTION DESIGN:
☆ ☆ ☆ ☆ ☆

MUSICAL SCORE:
☆ ☆ ☆ ☆ ☆

COSTUMING AND PROPS:
☆ ☆ ☆ ☆ ☆

NOTES:

TITLE:

YEAR:

GENRE:

WHERE WATCHED:

DATE SEEN:

WHO WITH:

OVERALL SCORE:
☆ ☆ ☆ ☆ ☆

DIRECTOR:
☆ ☆ ☆ ☆ ☆

CAST:
☆ ☆ ☆ ☆ ☆

SCREENPLAY:
☆ ☆ ☆ ☆ ☆

CINEMATOGRAPHY:
☆ ☆ ☆ ☆ ☆

SPECIAL EFFECTS/ANIMATION:
☆ ☆ ☆ ☆ ☆

PRODUCTION DESIGN:
☆ ☆ ☆ ☆ ☆

MUSICAL SCORE:
☆ ☆ ☆ ☆ ☆

COSTUMING AND PROPS:
☆ ☆ ☆ ☆ ☆

NOTES:

TITLE:

YEAR:

GENRE:

WHERE WATCHED:

DATE SEEN:

WHO WITH:

OVERALL SCORE:
☆ ☆ ☆ ☆ ☆

DIRECTOR:
☆ ☆ ☆ ☆ ☆

CAST:
☆ ☆ ☆ ☆ ☆

SCREENPLAY:
☆ ☆ ☆ ☆ ☆

CINEMATOGRAPHY:
☆ ☆ ☆ ☆ ☆

SPECIAL EFFECTS/ANIMATION:
☆ ☆ ☆ ☆ ☆

PRODUCTION DESIGN:
☆ ☆ ☆ ☆ ☆

MUSICAL SCORE:
☆ ☆ ☆ ☆ ☆

COSTUMING AND PROPS:
☆ ☆ ☆ ☆ ☆

NOTES:

TITLE:

YEAR:

GENRE:

WHERE WATCHED:

DATE SEEN:

WHO WITH:

OVERALL SCORE:
☆☆☆☆☆

DIRECTOR:
☆☆☆☆☆

CAST:
☆☆☆☆☆

SCREENPLAY:
☆☆☆☆☆

CINEMATOGRAPHY:
☆☆☆☆☆

SPECIAL EFFECTS/ANIMATION:
☆☆☆☆☆

PRODUCTION DESIGN:
☆☆☆☆☆

MUSICAL SCORE:
☆☆☆☆☆

COSTUMING AND PROPS:
☆☆☆☆☆

NOTES:

TITLE:

YEAR:

GENRE:

WHERE WATCHED:

DATE SEEN:

WHO WITH:

OVERALL SCORE:
☆ ☆ ☆ ☆ ☆

DIRECTOR:
☆ ☆ ☆ ☆ ☆

CAST:
☆ ☆ ☆ ☆ ☆

SCREENPLAY:
☆ ☆ ☆ ☆ ☆

CINEMATOGRAPHY:
☆ ☆ ☆ ☆ ☆

SPECIAL EFFECTS/ANIMATION:
☆ ☆ ☆ ☆ ☆

PRODUCTION DESIGN:
☆ ☆ ☆ ☆ ☆

MUSICAL SCORE:
☆ ☆ ☆ ☆ ☆

COSTUMING AND PROPS:
☆ ☆ ☆ ☆ ☆

NOTES:

TITLE:

YEAR:

GENRE:

WHERE WATCHED:

DATE SEEN:

WHO WITH:

OVERALL SCORE:
☆ ☆ ☆ ☆ ☆

DIRECTOR:
☆ ☆ ☆ ☆ ☆

CAST:
☆ ☆ ☆ ☆ ☆

SCREENPLAY:
☆ ☆ ☆ ☆ ☆

CINEMATOGRAPHY:
☆ ☆ ☆ ☆ ☆

SPECIAL EFFECTS/ANIMATION:
☆ ☆ ☆ ☆ ☆

PRODUCTION DESIGN:
☆ ☆ ☆ ☆ ☆

MUSICAL SCORE:
☆ ☆ ☆ ☆ ☆

COSTUMING AND PROPS:
☆ ☆ ☆ ☆ ☆

NOTES:

TITLE:

YEAR:

GENRE:

WHERE WATCHED:

DATE SEEN:

WHO WITH:

OVERALL SCORE:
☆ ☆ ☆ ☆ ☆

DIRECTOR:
☆ ☆ ☆ ☆ ☆

CAST:
☆ ☆ ☆ ☆ ☆

SCREENPLAY:
☆ ☆ ☆ ☆ ☆

CINEMATOGRAPHY:
☆ ☆ ☆ ☆ ☆

SPECIAL EFFECTS/ANIMATION:
☆ ☆ ☆ ☆ ☆

PRODUCTION DESIGN:
☆ ☆ ☆ ☆ ☆

MUSICAL SCORE:
☆ ☆ ☆ ☆ ☆

COSTUMING AND PROPS:
☆ ☆ ☆ ☆ ☆

NOTES:

TITLE:

YEAR:

GENRE:

WHERE WATCHED:

DATE SEEN:

WHO WITH:

OVERALL SCORE:
☆ ☆ ☆ ☆ ☆

DIRECTOR:
☆ ☆ ☆ ☆ ☆

CAST:
☆ ☆ ☆ ☆ ☆

SCREENPLAY:
☆ ☆ ☆ ☆ ☆

CINEMATOGRAPHY:
☆ ☆ ☆ ☆ ☆

SPECIAL EFFECTS/ANIMATION:
☆ ☆ ☆ ☆ ☆

PRODUCTION DESIGN:
☆ ☆ ☆ ☆ ☆

MUSICAL SCORE:
☆ ☆ ☆ ☆ ☆

COSTUMING AND PROPS:
☆ ☆ ☆ ☆ ☆

NOTES:

TITLE: **YEAR:**

GENRE:

WHERE WATCHED: **DATE SEEN:**

WHO WITH: **OVERALL SCORE:**

☆ ☆ ☆ ☆ ☆

DIRECTOR: ☆ ☆ ☆ ☆ ☆

CAST: ☆ ☆ ☆ ☆ ☆

SCREENPLAY: ☆ ☆ ☆ ☆ ☆

CINEMATOGRAPHY: ☆ ☆ ☆ ☆ ☆

SPECIAL EFFECTS/ANIMATION: ☆ ☆ ☆ ☆ ☆

PRODUCTION DESIGN: ☆ ☆ ☆ ☆ ☆

MUSICAL SCORE: ☆ ☆ ☆ ☆ ☆

COSTUMING AND PROPS: ☆ ☆ ☆ ☆ ☆

NOTES:

TITLE:

YEAR:

GENRE:

WHERE WATCHED:

DATE SEEN:

WHO WITH:

OVERALL SCORE:
☆ ☆ ☆ ☆ ☆

DIRECTOR:
☆ ☆ ☆ ☆ ☆

CAST:
☆ ☆ ☆ ☆ ☆

SCREENPLAY:
☆ ☆ ☆ ☆ ☆

CINEMATOGRAPHY:
☆ ☆ ☆ ☆ ☆

SPECIAL EFFECTS/ANIMATION:
☆ ☆ ☆ ☆ ☆

PRODUCTION DESIGN:
☆ ☆ ☆ ☆ ☆

MUSICAL SCORE:
☆ ☆ ☆ ☆ ☆

COSTUMING AND PROPS:
☆ ☆ ☆ ☆ ☆

NOTES:

TITLE:

YEAR:

GENRE:

WHERE WATCHED:

DATE SEEN:

WHO WITH:

OVERALL SCORE:
☆ ☆ ☆ ☆ ☆

DIRECTOR:
☆ ☆ ☆ ☆ ☆

CAST:
☆ ☆ ☆ ☆ ☆

SCREENPLAY:
☆ ☆ ☆ ☆ ☆

CINEMATOGRAPHY:
☆ ☆ ☆ ☆ ☆

SPECIAL EFFECTS/ANIMATION:
☆ ☆ ☆ ☆ ☆

PRODUCTION DESIGN:
☆ ☆ ☆ ☆ ☆

MUSICAL SCORE:
☆ ☆ ☆ ☆ ☆

COSTUMING AND PROPS:
☆ ☆ ☆ ☆ ☆

NOTES:

TITLE:

YEAR:

GENRE:

WHERE WATCHED:

DATE SEEN:

WHO WITH:

OVERALL SCORE:
☆ ☆ ☆ ☆ ☆

DIRECTOR:
☆ ☆ ☆ ☆ ☆

CAST:
☆ ☆ ☆ ☆ ☆

SCREENPLAY:
☆ ☆ ☆ ☆ ☆

CINEMATOGRAPHY:
☆ ☆ ☆ ☆ ☆

SPECIAL EFFECTS/ANIMATION:
☆ ☆ ☆ ☆ ☆

PRODUCTION DESIGN:
☆ ☆ ☆ ☆ ☆

MUSICAL SCORE:
☆ ☆ ☆ ☆ ☆

COSTUMING AND PROPS:
☆ ☆ ☆ ☆ ☆

NOTES:

TITLE:

YEAR:

GENRE:

WHERE WATCHED:

DATE SEEN:

WHO WITH:

OVERALL SCORE:
☆ ☆ ☆ ☆ ☆

DIRECTOR:
☆ ☆ ☆ ☆ ☆

CAST:
☆ ☆ ☆ ☆ ☆

SCREENPLAY:
☆ ☆ ☆ ☆ ☆

CINEMATOGRAPHY:
☆ ☆ ☆ ☆ ☆

SPECIAL EFFECTS/ANIMATION:
☆ ☆ ☆ ☆ ☆

PRODUCTION DESIGN:
☆ ☆ ☆ ☆ ☆

MUSICAL SCORE:
☆ ☆ ☆ ☆ ☆

COSTUMING AND PROPS:
☆ ☆ ☆ ☆ ☆

NOTES:

Made in the USA
San Bernardino, CA
06 December 2019